THE MAN BODY & MAN SOUL & MAN SPIRIT

By Rosalind Solomon

JANUARY 1, 2016
1ST EDITIION

Yahweh Abba God, I ask you to shield and protect EVERY reader of this book and give him or her a very clear understanding of all that you have directed me to write about in this book. I thank you, in the MIGTHY name of Yahushua Jesus Christ our Lord

"What then? shall we sin because we are not under the law, but under grace? God forbid. Know ye not, that to whom ye yield yourselves servants to obey, his servants ye are to whom ye obey; whether of sin unto death, or of obedience unto righteousness?"
Romans 6:15-16 6

"My people are destroyed for lack of knowledge ..."
Hosea 4:6
"But if our gospel be hiding, it is hiding to them that are lost: In whom the god of this world hath blinded the minds of them which believe not, lest the light of the glorious

gospel of Christ, who is the image of God, should shine

unto them. "I Corinthians 4:3-4 (important) God place this word here in a strange way I saw it typing and it was not me On Dec 22 2015 He was trying to tell me I was important to him and this book was important for his sheep be bless in Yah Jesus name.

12-21-+15 it is the word important

"here shall not be found among you any one that market his son or his daughter to pass through the fire [a form of human sacrifice to a demon], or that used divination, or an observer of times, or an enchanter, or a witch, or a charmer, or a consulter with familiar spirits, or a wizard, or a necromancer. For all That I do these things are an abomination unto the Lord: and because of these abominations the Lord thy God doth drive them out from before thee."

Deuteronomy 18:10-12.

"What? know ye not that he which is joined to a harlot is one body? for two, saith he, shall be one flesh ... Flee fornication. Every sin that a man doeth is without the body; but he that commiteth fornication sinneth against his own body."

I Corinthians 6:16 & 18

The word fornication means any sexual intercourse between a man and woman who are

not married to each other. (Definition from Vine's Expository Dictionary of New

Corinthians 7:12-16:

"If any brother hath a wife that believeth not, and she be pleased to dwell with

him, let him not put her away. And the woman which hath a husband that

believeth not, and if he be pleased to dwell with her, let her not leave him. For the

unbelieving husband is sanctified by the wife, and the unbelieving wife is

sanctified by the husband: else were your children unclean; but now are they holy.

But if the unbelieving depart, let him depart. A brother or a sister is not under

bondage in such cases: but God hath called us to peace. For what knowest thou, O

wife, whether thou shalt save thy husband? or how knowest thou, O man,

ROSALIND SOLOMON

whether thou shalt save thy wife?"

In such cases, the Christian spouse need only ask the Lord to sanctify their marriage bed and their unbelieving spouse and close that doorway with the blood of Jesus so that the believing spouse will not become infested with demons from the other through them

sexual intercourse

Any involvement in the Eastern religions such as T.M. (Transcendental Meditation), Yoga, etc., will result in demonic infestation and/or bondage. Careful study comparing the teachings of any cult with God's word will quickly show their errors. Most of the Eastern religions involve meditation. The topic of meditation is much misunderstood by most Christians and Satan has authored much deceptive literature on meditation posing as Christian literature. There are a numbers of references in scripture to meditation, but there is a very big difference between Godly meditation and Satanic meditation. Here are the basic principles here.

One of the major scripture references to meditation is found in Joshua 1:8: This book of the law shall not depart out of thy mouth; but thou shalt meditate therein day and night, that thou mays observe to do according to all that is written therein: for then thou shalt make thy way prosperous, and then thou shalt have good success wish to emphasize that the meditation referred to in this scripture involved the active reading, learning and memorizing of God's law given to the Israelites. Joshua was to learn the law so well that it would become a part of him. David followed the same principle —he wrote about it in

Psalm 119:9-11:

"Wherewithal shall a young man cleanse his way? By taking heed thereto according to thy word. With my whole heart have I sought thee: O let me not wander from thy commandments. Thy word have I hid in mine heart, that I might not sin against thee. Here again David was actively doing something — that is, learning and memorizing God's law so that he would not depart from it. At no time in scripture is meditation something passive. Satanic meditation is passive. Satan wants men to blank out their minds, attempt to clear their minds of all thoughts. This directly opens a door for demonic entrance and influence, because the simple fact is that God commands us to control our every thought, AND blank out our minds! If you don't control your mind, Satan will.

"For though we walk in the flesh, we do not war after the flesh: For the weapons

of our warfare are not carnal, but mighty through God to the pulling down of

strong holds; casting down imaginations, and every high thing [thoughts, in other

translations] that exalted itself against the knowledge of God, and bringing into

captivity every thought to the obedience of Christ." II Corinthians 10:3-5

"Thou wilt keep him in perfect peace, whose mind is stayed on thee ..." Isaiah

26:3
"[Jesus speaking] But when ye pray, use not vain repetitions, as the heathen do ..."

"Matthew 6:7" But shun profane and vain babblings: for they will increase unto

more ungodliness." II Timothy 2:16

There is a dangerous teaching in some charismatic churches where members are told to repeat a certain phrase over and over, or to "blank out their minds and let the Holy Spirit take over." (This is especially done in reference to an effort to get someone to speak in tongues.) Any kind of blank mind will be taken over by a spirit alright, but unfortunately, an unholy spirit not the Holy Spirit. Demons and demonic bondage are inherited. The doorway of inheritance is an often overlooked one. Although we are no longer under the old law because of the new covenant in Yah Christ's blood, we can find some very important scriptures and principles by studying the Old Testament. We must also bear in mind that any sin not brought under Yah Jesus Christ's blood is legal ground for Satan and his demon's. There are many references in the Old Testament to the sins of the fathers being passed down to the sons. Some are found in Exodus 20:5, 34:7, Numbers 14:18 '

Deuteronomy 5:9. Exodus 34:6-7 says:

"And the Lord passed by before him, and proclaimed, The Lord, The Lord God,

merciful and gracious, longsuffering, and abundant in goodness and truth,

keeping mercy for thousands, forgiving iniquity and transgression and sin, and

that will by no means clear the guilty; visiting the iniquity of the fathers upon the children, and upon the children's children, unto the third and to the fourth

generation."

We also find that every time there was a major revival in Israel, the people came together

in fasting and prayer not only to confess their own sins, but the sins of their fathers also.

Nehemiah 9:1-2:

"Now in the twenty and fourth day of this month the children of Israel were

assembled with fasting, and with sack clothes, and earth upon them. And the seed

of Israel separated themselves from all strangers, and stood and confessed them

sins, and the iniquities [sins or evil deeds] of their fathers."

Other references are II Chronicles 29:1-11 during the reign gnat of King Hezekiah, II

Chronicles 34: 19-21, and many other references as well.

(I Corinthians 10:14-21), any demonic infestation, any oaths taken by

parents or ancestors which are binding upon descendants (as are most occult, pagan,

Mormon, Masonic oaths) etc.

One of Satan's and his cohorts and demon's biggest tools in our country today is the occult role-playing fantasy games made and created by Satan, which have become so popular. Satan is using these games to produce a vast army of the most intelligent young people in this country; an army that the Anti-Christ will be able to tap into and control in an instant. Through their involvement in these games, people can be controlled demonically without them ever realizing what is going on with them. In many states such games are used as a part of the school curriculum for the more intelligent students.

Almost every school has extracurricular clubs formed to play the games. In essence, such games are crash courses in witchcraft. Unfortunately, the participants usually do not realize this until it is too late players are supposed to "visualize" the action of the game in their minds. The better they become at "seeing" the action and therefore anticipating and looking for the moves of the various "monsters", creature's and the other players, the more advanced they become in the game.

What people don't realize at first is that these monsters are actually real demons. What they think they are visualizing in their minds; they are in actuality beginning to see in the spirit world. The better they become at "seeing" in the game, the more in-tune and connected they are with the spirit world. The imagination is a key stepping stone to contact with the spirit world. the demons will come and talk to them, and tell them they gain more power if they, invite the more intelligent of the demons to come into them. Christians have lost interest in the Yahweh God as a result of playing theses game's so many numbers of people will never come to a saving knowledge of Jesus because of the demonic bondage they have come under by playing these games.

Also Occultist influences are on the rampant rise in toys for small children as well as the cartoons on TV. Small children are naturally very imaginative. Satan knows that if he can direct their imagination to the spirit world they will quickly learn to see and communicate with his demons. Parents need to be extremely wise careful what toys they permit their little ones to play with, and what cartoons they permit them to watch on TV also know this do not overlook power witches' cartoons that are taught on T, V. Also Christians should never have anything to do with biofeedback. It is nothing more than modernized Yoga, satanic meditation and witchcraft.

Another area often overlooked, but is very powerful, is that of rock music. Rock music   and R and B music is Satan's music. Like so many other things, the whole movement of rock music and R and B music was carefully planned and carried out by Satan and his servants from its very beginning. R and B and Rock music didn't "just happen," it was a carefully masterminded plan by none other than Satan himself.

Music Industry Satanic Alter to Satan

Special ceremonies at various recording studios throughout the America is used for the special specific purpose of placing satanic blessings on the rock music recorded and r and b music and certain Jazz and Country music. THE Witches usually 13 of them, high powered one's do incantations which placed is demons on EVERY record and CD of rock music and R and B music RECORD CD SOLD. I Speak about this more in my book called *SERCET TO DESTROYING WITCHCRAFT IN THE CHURCH*. Publish on amazon.com Sometimes they also called up special demons who was speaking on the recordings —especially in the various back masked messages.

Also, in many, of the recordings, the Satanists themselves were also recorded in the background *(masked by the over-all noise of the music)*. So you cannot hear them doing all of the chants and incantations to summon up stronger demon's every time one of the records or cd or videos is played. As the music is played, these demons are called into the room to afflict the one who is playing the music and anyone else who is listening. The purpose of all of this? Is Mind control! Mind control not only to give the listeners understanding of the messages about Satan conveyed to them by the music, but also to stop the person from recognizing their need for Yah Jesus and the salvation He died on the cavalry for them.

ALSO TO give Many of the song lyrics are themselves actual incantations calling up demons when the song is sung OR HEARD. The purpose of this is DOUBEL fold to exert control over the one who is the listener and to provide the listener with an actual incantation he or she can use to send demons upon another person. This is done to gain revenge by Satan and demons afflicting them with illness, accidents, etc. And also to help influence another person into the bondage.

All these doorways must be closed.

"If we confess our sins, he is faithful and just to forgive us our sins, and to

cleanse us from all unrighteousness." I John 1:9.

If you have participated or been involved in any way of these things, you can close the door by praying "Yahweh Abba of Heaven, I confess to you my involvement in _____. I realize that such a thing(s) is this is an abomination to you and detestable in your sight. I humbly seek and   ask your forgiveness for my s all my in in this area(s) and I seek for geneses for my Ancestor too going all the way back to Adam and Eve on My father and mother and step parents side if you have any. I ask you to lift out any demonic entrance as the result of my actions and my ancestor to cleanse me from my sins and close the doorway(s)now and forever more with the precious blood of Yahushua Jesus. I ask for this and thank you for it, in Yah Jesus' name."

Prayer to Stop Listening to the Satanic Order of Satan Music

"Satan and your demons and witches, I have asked my Yahweh heavenly Father for forgiveness for

participating in _____ and have received it. I now by faith close the doorway of all of those

 area of my life to you forever through the blood of Yah Jesus Christ shed on the

cavalry for me. In the name of Yah Jesus I command you to go away!"

"But if our gospel be hiding, it is hiding to them that are lost: In

whom the god of this world hath blinded the minds of

them which believe not, lest the light of the glorious

gospel of Christ, who is the image of God, should shine

unto them."

II Corinthians 4:3-4

The Spirit of the Lord God is upon me; ... to proclaim

liberty to the captives, and the opening of the prison to

them that are bound."

Isaiah 61:1

Short lesson

Demons can get in that can inhabit the body, soul, and spirit, all at the same time. Especially Incubus and succubus Marine Kingdom Demon's.

He has thousands of tentacles Snake incubus which he wants and entwines deep down into his subordinates, THESES DEONS CAN HAVE A doorway — to inheritance. At the death of a family member or from an ancestor. They will transfer at the death of the family member to the one who is a carnal saint or not a saint at all. The powerful demons that inhabited Him or her will be passed on to another member of the family each area

Theses Marine demon will try to slammed shut the door in woman OR MAN SPIRIT so that she could no longer sense God's presence The spirit man will be dead completely to God at that time in a person life, unless the spirit can get through to them in time before they die and perish. See if the holy spirit can get in to the spirit to remove the power demon blocking the soul from the spirit. Then the growth of the Holy Spirit can and will take-over. The Holy Spirit is something that THESES DEMONS CANNOT STAND OR TAKE.

They cannot tolerate The Holy spirit growth in the person from seeking God so Incubus and Succubus and any power demon will do all they can to prevent the spirit from getting to the soul. The spirit man is supposed to be over powering the soul not the other way around. This is why Satan have his human cohorts tap in to the Latten Power of their soul, so they can block the spirit weaken it so to speak from getting to through the soul. There for winning them back to God. This is why Satanic folks cannot come to God the spirit has been weaken by a power demon BY BEING BLOCK BY THE DEMON. Also the soul has been block and is in bondage held hostage to the demons. Then the spirit man comes in to agreement with the demons and then that is worst for the person. So this is why the demons and Satan do all this to have the person turn away from God it will tried to turn away from one commitment to the Yahweh God.

Hosea 4:6 which

says, "My people are destroyed for lack of knowledge

Break Inheritance lines to Soul Heart Mind and Spirit and Body Prayer

IN the Mighty Name of Yah Jesus Father God Yahweh. I repent for my ancestor who open theses door ways to theses demons Incubus and Succubus and Satan and Eldora Night mare demons and Fear demons and Familiar spirits demons and the suborders and tentacle demons. I ask you to forgive them going all the way back to Adam and Eve on my father and mother side and step parents this is only if you had any. I ask you to wash our sins and their sins under the blood of Yahushua Jesus now and forever more. In Yah Jesus name

I also ask You Yahweh father in Yah Jesus name to cut the soul line and inheriting line from our ancestor spirit and soul. heart and mind the brain and bones and blood and sexual organs and hair on our head and body and our eyes. So that we may be free and serve you whole heartily with no hinderers any more from Satan and his kingdom. I cancel and void out all effect and manifestations and the inheriting curse on my blood line and lineage and DNA and

Genes and Foundation and the soul of our Generation and the Spirit of our Generation and the mind of our generation and The body of our Generation with the blood of Yah Jesus. In Yah Jesus name. These things of Satan no longer exists in our family line any more. Now all of us will have the choice and opportunity to come back to you and serve you and live for you father in Yah Jesus name. I ask that You Yahweh and The Holy Spirit and Yah Jesus impart in us and fill us up and seal all of you in us and us in you all forever more sealed in the blood of Yah Jesus. So Satan and demons cannot ever have controls over us again nor our blood line or DNA or take any more souls to hell from this generation or Blood line again in Yahushua Jesus name.

PRAYER TO BOUND DEMONS SO YOU CAN GET ANY ONE TO HEAR YOU TELL THEM ABOUT YAH JESUS SALVATION

. Hear me "You demons binding____, I take authority over you in the name of Yah Jesus Christ my Lord and savior. I bind you in the name of Yah Jesus, you may not afflict ____ today. My house is committed to the Lord and is holy ground. You are a trespasser and may not function here. I bind you and command you to leave in the name of Yah Jesus!" and you are forbidden and disallowed to ever come back in yah Jesus name

For people out of your household and when Evangelizing

Say same prayer except add in deepening on who you are witnessing to in Yah Jesus name

You can ask the Lord to let you "stand in the gap" for the unsaved person.

. See Ezekiel 22:30-31. Ask the Lord to let you stand in the gap for this person in order that their eyes may be opened and their will

set free to accept ah Jesus., you must understand the wonderful position of power our Lord Jesus has placed us in. Hebrews says:

"Let us therefore come boldly unto the throne of

grace, that we may obtain mercy, and find grace to help in time of need." Hebrews

4:16 S

Scripture shows us that Satan comes before God and petitions Him for people. The account given in Job chapter 1 clearly demonstrates this. Also Satan obviously petitioned God for Peter.

"And the Lord said, Simon, Simon, behold, Satan hath desired to have you, that

he may sift you as wheat: But I have prayed for thee, that thy faith fails not: and

when thou are converted, strengthen thy brethren." Luke 22:31-32

Satan is not finally thrown out of heaven until the 12th chapter of Revelation

"And there was war in heaven: Michael and his angels fought against the dragon;

and the dragon fought and his angels, and prevailed not; neither was their place

found any more in heaven. And the great dragon was cast out, that old serpent,

called the Devil, and Satan, which deceiveth the whole world: he was cast out into

the earth, and his angels were cast out with him. And I heard a loud voice saying in heaven, now is come salvation, and strength, and the kingdom of God, and the

power of his Christ: for the accuser of our brethren is cast down, which accused

them before our God day and night." Revelation 12:7-10

You must understand that Satan stands before the throne of God petitioning our heavenly YAHWEH Father for our unsaved loved ones. Satan points the accusing finger and says, "See, so-and-so Is participating in this or that (or whatever), therefore I have a legal right to his/her soul and to influence his/her life and to send my demons into him/her. "Because God is absolutely just, He must grant Satan his petition if it is uncontested. But we as heirs and joint heirs with Jesus Christ have more right to petition God the Father than Satan does. We must "boldly" go before the throne and counter-petition Satan. We can pray something like this:

Prayer to Petition a Counter Petition Against Satan for Love One's

. Yahweh "God and Father, I do so counter-petition Satan. I come to you in the name of Yahushua Jesus Christ my Lord and savior and I lay claim to this person. Say their name or names_____ I claim him/her as my inheritance

which you promised to give to me (if the person is your child, or spouse). Satan may not have him/her. I ask you to open his/her eyes so that they can see the light of the gospel of Yah Jesus Christ."

I sealed this in the blood of Yah Jesus and invoke the blood of the lamb around them so Satan and his Demons and evil Kingdom cannot and will not steal this prayer from them in Yah Jesus name.

Note This --- If the person you are petitioning for is not a relative, you can petition on the basis that

Jesus Christ commanded us to make disciples of the whole world and we can claim that

person for a disciple of Jesus Christ.

And the very God of peace sanctify you wholly; and I pray God your whole spirit

and soul and body be preserved blameless unto the coming of our Lord Jesus

Christ." I Thessalonians 5:23.

Paul teaches us here that we as humans are tripartite beings. That is, we have three separate parts — the body, the soul (which is our conscious intellect, will, and emotions), and the spirit. He plainly states that all three must be cleansed and committed to Jesus, and that Jesus himself must enable us to keep all three parts "blameless" until His return.

Genesis 2:7 says,

"And the Lord God formed man of the dust of the ground, and breathed into his

nostrils the breath of life; and man became a living soul."

That is, Adam lived, and became aware of himself. In essence our self is our soul which manifests in our mind, our will, and our emotions.

"There is a natural body and there is a spiritual body." I Corinthians 15:44

This is a much overlooked verse. Our spirits have a form or shape, a body corresponding to our physical body. Few people other than the Satanists or those involved in such things as astral projection realizes this

"I knew a man in Christ, (whether in the body, cannot

tell; or whether out of the body, I cannot tell: God knoweth;) such a one caught

up to the third heaven. And I knew such a man, (whether in the body, or out of

the body, I cannot tell: God knoweth;) How that he was caught up into paradise,

and heard unspeakable words, which it is not lawful for a man to utter." II

Corinthians 12:2-4

"After this I looked, and, behold, a door was opened in heaven: and the first voice

which I heard was as it were of a trumpet talking with me; which said, come up

hither, and I will shew thee things which must be hereafter. And immediately I

was in the spirit: and, behold, a throne was set in heaven, and one sat on the

throne." Revelation 4:1-2

These scriptures and others show an experience perceived in the person's spirit, and that the spirit body was separated from the physical body. Notice that when John stated that The was in the "spirit" that it is spelled with a small's" signifying his own human spirit.

Every time the Holy Spirit is referred to in scripture it is spelled with a capital "S" as in

Revelation 1:10:

"I was in the Spirit on the Lord's day, and heard behind

me a great voice, as of a trumpet..." "For the word of

God is quick, and powerful, and sharper than any two-edged

sword, piercing even to the dividing asunder of

soul and spirit, ..."

Hebrews 4:12

Did you ever wonder and think about why it is necessary to divide between our soul and spirit? According to the above verse there can be a division made (or separation of) the soul and the spirit. This is what Satan did when they ate the poison of the tree of good and evil in the Garden of Eden.

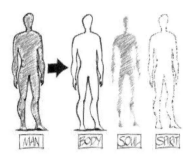

See the Holy Spirit comes in at rebirth when we accept Yah Jesus as our Lord and Savior, our spiritual body is re-born, or rejuvenated so that we can commune with and worship Yah Jesus as Adam did before the fall. The fact that it is through our human spirit that we commune with God (with the help of the Holy Spirit) is for sure show us in the Bible in scripture

"[Jesus is speaking] But the hour cometh, and now is,

when the true worshipers shall worship the Father in

spirit and in truth: for the Father seeketh such to worship

him. God is a Spirit: and they that worship him must

worship him in spirit and in truth."

John 4:23-24

Now the Angels are also clearly defined in the Bible as being spirits:

"Who [referring to God] maketh his angel's spirits;"

Psalm 104:4

This verse is also quoted by Paul in Hebrews 1:7.

"But to which of the angels said he at any time, Sit on me

right hand, until I make thine enemies thy footstool? Are

they not all ministering spirits, sent forth to minister for

them who shall be heirs of salvation?" Hebrews 1:13-14

Now Satan and his demons are as well spirits being, they were once angels in God's service until they rebelled. Yahushua Jesus himself defines these creatures as angels and thus spirits. One scripture reference for this is in

Matthew 25:41:

"Then shall he say also unto them on the left hand, depart from me, ye cursed,

into everlasting fire, prepared for the devil and his angels." Matthew 25:41

So now you know from these scriptures and many others that not only is God a Spirit, but there are certainly other spirit beings as well and angels — some in God's service, some in Satan's service of him. Our spiritual bodies are the link between us and the spirit world because the spirit world cannot be seen or measured with anything physical.

Through the Holy Spirit, our spirits are able to commune with and worship God, but the scripture in Hebrews 4:12 shows us that it is not God's will for us to regain the conscious control of our spirit bodies while we remain here on the earth in our sinful condition. This is why the sword of the Spirit severs between the soul and spirit. Once this severing has taken place the soul (mind, intellect, will) can no longer control the spirit body. Thesis also why the Lord is so adamant in I Thessalonians 5:23 that our spirit must be under the total mastership of Yahushua Jesus Christ, as well as our soul and physical body.

There is an intriguing scripture in Revelation 18:11 & 13:
There is a difference made between bodies and souls of Humans because there is phenomenal amount of certain power and special intelligence in the spirit bodies of humans being especially when those spirit bodies are under the control of their soul. Satan has been working seriously and vastly through the ages since the fall of Adam and Eve to gain the use of these spiritual bodies for his own evil schemes A physical bodies OF A Human are very weak and really are of little use to Satan, but their spiritual bodies under the conscious control of their souls, are very different. Satan's goal is to teach humans to again regain the conscious control of their spiritual bodies. Many do. Once this is achieved, these people can perceive the spirit world as well as the physical world.

They can talk freely with demons, leave their physical bodies with their spirit bodies, and with full conscious awareness go places and do things with, what seems to the average human, supernatural power. This is why witches etc. have power it is not the power of Satan and demons it is power God has already place in us. Satan and demons just add to it with their demonic powers to pollute diluted and devilled and weaken it and us to be used to serve their evil means and to destroy man kind and then their souls to hell fire. Satan and his kingdom wants mankind to suffer their same fate they miss God an d heaven so they feel we should too. There is a special class of demons, I learned about who refer to themselves as "power demons "who seem to provide the "glue" so to speak, to establish the link between the soul and spirit body enabling the person involved to gain conscious control of his spirit body. The imagination is a key stepping stone to develop the link between soul and spirit. That is why it is so important to bring every thought into captivity to Christ (2 Cor. 10:3-5). Theses demons as so get in the human when any procession of demons come in a human many do not know this. This is a very overlooked area in deliverance and this doorway IS MOST OF THE TIME LEFT OPEN. The result OF THIS IS MUCH suffering as Satan and his demons will continuously harass the person. If the person being so tormented will simply pray and ask the Lord to remove all their ability to perceive the spirit world and ask the Lord to sever between his soul and spirit (as in Hebrews 4:12), they will gain tremendous relief from such torment by the evil spirit world. After this the person will perceive the spirit world only when the Lord chooses to give them such perception. Their spirit will, from that point on, be totally under the mastership of Jesus Christ.

Prayer to do Just That

Father Yahweh I ask you to go all the way back to my Ancestor back to Adam and Eve on my mother and father side and step parents if person have any. And remove all of their Satan and his Demons and itches warlocks and Wizard, Sorcerer, and all Satan Elect and Printability and heavenly host that fell with Satan. Take away their Ability to perceive me or family members and children and spouse in the spirit and spiritual world. In The Mighty name of Yahushua Jesus. Father Yahweh server the, lines, cords, ropes, chains, cable, roots astral line, spiritual line any and every thing they are or may be using to be able to perceive us in the spirit or spiritual world. Server it all now Father Yahweh with your fire and the blood of the Lamb. Yah Jesus the King of KING and Salvation Name for ever more. Forever and eternity in Yah Jesus name Lord to take complete control of our spirits. In Yah Jesus name

Very Important Scripture on Soul and the Spirit Man That are over look in The churches today.

"His spirit was troubled" Gen. 41.8

"Then their spirit was appeased toward him" Judges 8.3 Darby

"He that is hasty of spirit exalteth folly" Prov. 14.29 Darby

"A downcast spirit dries up the bones" Prov. 17.22

"Those who err in spirit" Is. 29.24

"And shall wail for anguish of spirit" Is. 65.14

"His spirit was hardened" Dan. 5.20

The Soul's Faculty of Volition

"Give me not up to the will (original, "soul") of my adversaries" Ps. 27.12

"Thou dost not give him up to the will (original, "soul") of his enemies"

Ps. 41.2

"Delivered you to the greed (original, "soul") of your enemies" Ezek.

16.27

"You shall let her go where she will (original, "soul")" Deut. 21.14

"Aha, we have our heart's desire (original, "soul")" Ps. 35.25

"Or swear an oath to bind himself (original, "soul") by a pledge" Num.

30.2

"Now set your mind and heart (original, "soul") to seek the Lord your

God" 1 Chron. 22.18

"They desire and lift up their soul to return to dwell there" Jer. 44.14

Amplified

"These afflictions my soul refuses to touch" Job 6.7 Amplified

Spirit and Soul 41

"My soul chooseth strangling, death, rather than my bones" Job 7.15

Darby

all, having their springs in the soul.

B) The Soul's Faculty of Intellect or Mind

"Whereunto they lift up their soul, their sons and their daughters" Ezek.

24.25 Darby

"That a soul be without knowledge is not good" Prov. 19.2 Darby

"How long must I bear pain (Syriac: Hebrew: hold counsels) in me soul?" Ps. 13.2

"Marvelous are thy works; and that my soul knoweth right well" Ps.

139.14 Darby

"My soul continually thinks of it" Lam. 3.20

"Knowledge will be pleasant to your soul" Prov. 2.10

"Keep sound wisdom and discretion . . . and they will be life for your

soul" Prov. 3.21,22

"Know that wisdom is such to your soul" Prov. 24.14

Here "knowledge," "counsel," "lift up," "think," etc., exist as the

activities of man's intellect or mind, which the Bible indicates as

emanating from the soul.

C) The Soul's Faculty of Emotion

1) EMOTIONS OF AFFECTION

"The soul of Jonathan was knit to the soul of David, and Jonathan

loved him as his own soul" 1 Sam. 18.1

"You whom my soul loves" Song 1.7

"My soul magnifies the Lord" Luke 1.46

"His life abhorreth bread, and his soul dainty food" Job 33.20 Darby

"Who are hated by David's soul" 2 Sam. 5.8

"My soul was vexed with them" Zech. 11.8 Darby

"You shall love the Lord your God . . . with all your soul" Deut. 6.5

"My soul is weary of my life" Job 10:1 Darby

"Their soul abhorreth all manner of food" Ps. 107:18 Darby

2) EMOTIONS OF DESIRE

42 The Spiritual Man

"For whatever thy soul desireth . . . or for whatever thy soul asketh

of thee" Deut. 14.26 Darby

"What thy soul may say" 1 Sam. 20.4 Darby

"My soul longs, yea, faints for the courts of the Lord" Ps. 84.2

"Your soul's longing" Ezek. 24.21 Darby

"So longs my soul for thee, O God" Ps. 42.1

"My soul yearns for thee in the night" Is. 26.9

"My soul is well pleased" Matt. 12.18

3) EMOTIONS OF FEELING AND SENSING

"A sword will pierce through your own soul also" Luke 2.35

"All the people were bitter in soul" 1 Sam. 30.6

"Her soul is bitter and vexed within her" 2 Kings 4.27 Amplified

"His soul was grieved for the misery of Israel" Judges 10.16 Darby

"How long will ye vex my soul" Job 19.2 Darby

"My soul shall exult in my God" Is. 61.10

"Gladden the soul of thy servant" Ps. 86.4

"Their soul fainted within them" Ps. 107.5

"Why are you cast down, O my soul" Ps. 42.5

"Return, O my soul, to your rest" Ps. 116.7

"My soul is consumed with longing" Ps. 119.20

"Sweetness to the soul" Prov. 16.24

"Let your soul delight itself in fatness" Is. 55.2 Amplified

"My soul fainted within me" Jonah 2.7

"My soul is very sorrowful" Matt. 26.38

"Now is my soul troubled" John 12.27

"He was vexed in his righteous soul day after day" 2 Peter 2.8

"You shall not defile yourselves with them" Lev. 11.43

"You shall not defile yourselves" Lev. 11.44

"For themselves and for their descendants" Esther 9.31

"You who tear yourself in your anger" Job 18.4

"He justified himself" Job 32.2

"But themselves go into captivity" Is. 46.2

"What every one (original, "every soul") must eat, that only may be

prepared by you" Ex. 12.16

"Who kills any person (original, "kill any soul") without intent" Num.

35.11,15

"Let me (original, "let my soul") die the death of the righteous" Num.

23.10

"When any one (original, "any soul") brings a cereal offering" Lev. 2.1

"I have . . . quieted myself" Ps. 131.2 AV

"Think not that in the king's palace you (original, "soul") will escape"

Esther 4.13

"The Lord God has sworn by himself (original, "sworn by his soul")"

Amos 6.8

This Good to Prayer before you Go to Bed the Full Armor Prayer of God for Night Time (Sleep)

No TV right before retiring for the evening! Read the Word if you like, read a Psalms, or pray.

The Full Armor Prayer of God for Night Time (Sleep)

No TV right before retiring for the evening! Read the Word if you like, read a Psalms, or pray.

Yahweh, Father in Heaven, as I go to bed, give me sweet rest. Yahweh, I place my spirit in your hands. Watch over me. Put a hedge of protection around me (and my children, grandchildren, and family). Watch over us Father, in Yahushua Name. Father, in the Name of Yahushua Jesus, I forbid any evil spirits from manipulating AND DEVILLING me in my dreams, from seeking to manipulate my destiny in my dreams or from feeding us demonic food to make us sick or innate us in their demonic kingdom in Yahushua Jesus' Name. Father, as You have commanded in Your Word, in Ephesians 6:12-17, I put on the full armor of You (helmet of salvation, breastplate of righteousness, belt of truth, sandals of the gospel of peace, shield of faith, and the Sword of the Spirit), Yahweh, on me, my children, grandchildren, spouse, and family members, in Yahushua Name. Yahweh, Abba God, Father, as I wear Your armor, and I place it on my family members, fight for me and fight for my family members, this night and every night. And as we wake in the morning, as You bless us, in Yahushua Ha Meshach, Jesus Christ, and Master's Name, sealed in the Blood of Yahushua.

So many Christians Sheep think that they must "blank out "in their Mind

So many Christians Sheep think that they must "have their mines completely blanked out" their minds so that the Holy Spirit can speak through them, or "take them over. The Bible clearly shows and tells us that we are to actively be in the battel with the with the Holy Spirit. WHEN EVER we blank out our minds, the spirit speaking through us is most Is not the Holy Spirit. So many Christians are, and have been, mislead because of their lack of knowledge of The laws and God's principles about their spirits. Many false prophecies given by people who blank out their minds thinking this gives control to the Holy Spirit are demonic prophecies. Too many Christians are misled in this area and accept such prophecies because the person prophesying knows facts about them or their life that they think only God could know. They forget that Satan knows every detail of our lives, the only thing he doesn't know is the thoughts and intentions of our hearts. There is a growing teaching the Christians of America which is very dangerous I learned this through studies That is, "Our soul man should be placed under the authority of our spiritual man because once indwelt by the Holy Spirit our spirits are without sin." HERE IS TWO things wrong with this DOCTRINE Now, the only way the soul can be placed under the authority of the spirit is to establish conscious contact between he soul and spirit.

This is pure witchcraft. I Peter 1:22 says: *"Seeing that ye have purified your souls in obeying the truth through the Spirit unto unfeigned love of the brethren...* See here that in this verse *"Spirit" is spelled with a capital "S" referring to the Holy Spirit. Our souls are "purified" by staying in subjection to and obeying the Holy Spirit, not our own human spirits. Second, I Thessalonians 5:23* clearly shows us that our spirits are vulnerable to fall into sin because Jesus must keep them blameless until His return. The keeping is an ongoing thing. See and read it again: *"And the very God of peace sanctify you wholly; and I pray God your whole spirit and soul and body be preserved blameless unto the coming of our Lord Jesus*

Christ." I Thessalonians 5:23

I John 1:8-9 certainly doesn't agree with this teaching. It says:

"If we say that we have no sin, we deceive ourselves, and the truth is not in us. If

we confess our sins, he is faithful and just to forgive us our sins, and to cleanse us

from all unrighteousness." I John 1:8-9

There is one other major area regarding our spirits that has a very terrible impact upon many people, but is not taught about in our churches. This is the fact that, whenever he has the chance, Satan will use a person's spirit body without his awareness. *This is considering to be hate of your brother to God oh mighty Yahweh.*

"Whosoever hateth his brother is a murderer ..."

I John 3:15

I often use to think about this verse before I could have understood the spirit body. How could one be a murderer through an emotion, hatred, if he did not physically do something to bring about the death of the person he hated? Hatred is a conscious sin. As such, it gives Satan legal ground in our lives if we permit it to dwell in our hearts for far too long with no remorse or repentance at all. If you hate someone, Satan can step in and use your spirit body to attack the person you hate.

Its giving him negative energy and material to build on and in you so he can do just that. Now such an attack from Satan can produce all sorts of illness, accident emotional problems, and even physical death. The person doing the hating usually is never aware that Satan is using his spirit body. The person being hated usually has no idea where his trouble is really coming from. That is why we must be so careful to ask Yah Jesus to cleanse and keep pure all three parts, body, soul, and spirit. That is why the Lord Jesus gave us so many commands to forgive one another. Forgiveness puts a stop to hatred. We Christians should ask the Lord regularly to clean out our hearts of any sin.

Prayer for Pureness of Body and Soul and Spirit and Heart and Mind Prayer

Abba Yahweh God I ask you this day to please wash my Heart and mind and body and soul and spirit in the blood of Yah Jesus in Yah Jesus name. and to Purified All of the members of you in me and on me with Fire of the Holy Spirit to burn out all Impurity in me I know of and I do not Know of Father Yahweh in Yahushua Jesus name. I ask You Yahweh Father to continually remind me to do this daily just as I have to place my Armor of You on Like it says in Ephesians 6 That I must place my Armor on every 24 hours. So I thank you father in advance for this and doing this for me in Yah Jesus name and for my Family as well in Yah Jesus name.

"Create in me a clean heart, O God; and renew a right spirit within me." Psalm

51:10

Again, please note the small "s" in the word spirit here. Obviously the sin in David's heart

had affected his spirit also.

Are you willing to stand in the gap for someone?

"And I sought for a man among them, that should make up the hedge, and standing the gap before me for the land, that I should not destroy it: but I found none.

Therefore, have I poured out mine indignation upon them; I have consumed them

with the fire of my wrath: their own way have I recompensed upon their heads,

saith the Lord God." Ezekiel 22:30-31

"Standing in the gap" can be done in several different ways. Often it is necessary to ask the Lord to let you stand in the gap for a particular person so that he can have an opportunity to hear the gospel free from demonic interference. Again remember II

Corinthians 4:3-4:

"But if our gospel be hiding, it is hiding to them that are lost: In whom the god of this

world hath blinded the minds of them which believe not, lest the light of the

glorious gospel of Christ, who is the image of God, should shine unto them."

In Ezekiel 22:30-32

God was looking for someone who would be willing to stand and fight Satan and his demons to stop them from blinding the people so that they could see their need for a savior. Because the YAH Jesus. Yahweh could not find such a person He said that He would have to pour out His wrath and punishment upon the people for their sins. Ultimately, Yahushua Jesus Christ is the ONE who stands in the gap for all sinners.

That is why He came to earth and died for the righteous chosen one of God Yahweh and him and the holy Spirit bearing the punishment for our sins. However, Yah Jesus set the example for us. We cannot pay the price for our sins or anyone else's, but we can fight hard for them. In that sense, I believe we can stand in the gap for them. We as Christian warriors of God must be willing to stand in the gap and fight in the spiritual realm to break the demonic forces blinding the unsaved. Paul makes it very clear in

Ephesians 6:12 that:

"For we wrestle not against flesh and blood, but against principalities, against

powers, against the rulers of the darkness of this world, against spiritual

wickedness in high places."

We often pray a prayer such as the following:

"Lord, please let me stand in the gap for and fight for him or her so that his eyes will be opened and he or she will be freed from demonic bondage so that he can see his need for Jesus. "The Lord has shown us yet another way to stand in the gap. Look at the following scriptures: "Is not this the fast that I have chosen? to lose the bands of wickedness, to undo the heavy burdens, and to let the oppressed go free, and that ye break every yoke?" Isaiah 58:6

"Bear ye one another's burdens, and so fulfill the law of Christ." *Galatians 6:2*

"Greater love hath no man than this, that a man lay down his life *for his friends."*

John 15:13

The above scriptures clearly show that the Lord Yah Jesus expects us to help bear the burdens and hurts of our Christian brothers and sisters and to fight whenever necessary to free them from oppression. Standing in the gap is one way of doing this. Let's make one thing clear. By standing in the gap you do NOT accept anything from the demons. Your purpose is to stand in the power of Yah Jesus Christ. You should not "accept" illness or any other form of oppression.

You must rebuke all demonic oppression in the name of Yah Jesus Christ and forbid it from afflicting you or the person you are fighting for. That is the reason and purpose of "standing in the gap" for our brother's and sister's. remember this you can't put yourself in the gap. Only the yah Jesus Christ the Lord can do that because only Yah Jesus the Lord controls your spirit body. What you must do is ask Father God Yahweh to put you there if it is within His will to do so. You must be willing to allow Father to use you in any way He wants for the benefit of another person. You cannot decide how you are to be used

Why Should We Fight back Satan and his kingdom?

Let us first look at what Yah Jesus Himself had to say about this subject when He was here on earth. We can go to a better source. "Think not that I am come to send peace on earth: I came not to send peace, but as word. For I am come to set a man at variance against his father, and the daughter against her mother, and the daughter-in-law against her mother-in-law. And adman's foes shall be they of his own household. He that loved father or mother more than me is not worthy of me: and he that loved son or daughter more than me is not worthy of me. And he that taketh not his cross, and followeth after me, is not worthy of me.

He that findeth his life shall lose it: and he that loseth his life

for my sake shall find it." Matthew 10:34-39

Please note where Yahushua Jesus said in verse 34 "Think not that I am come to send peace on earth: I came not to send peace, but a sword." This cuts directly across the "peace and love gospel" that is being taught so widely. Then in verse 39 Yah Jesus says "He that findeth this life shall lose it: and he that loseth his life for my sake shall find it." Christianity involves violence if we practice it the way God wants us to. Losing our lives does not *involve peaceful co-existence with the world.*

"Behold, I send you forth as sheep in the midst of wolves:

be ye therefore wise as serpents, and harmless as doves.

But beware of men: for they will deliver you up to the

councils, and they will scourge you in their synagogues;

And ye shall be brought before governors and kings for
my sake, for a testimony against them and the Gentiles.
But when they deliver you up, take no thought how or
what ye shall speak: for it shall be given you in that same
hour what ye shall speak.

For it is not ye that speak, but
the Spirit of your Father which speaketh in you. And the
brother shall deliver up the brother to death, and the
father the child: and the children shall rise up against their
parents, and cause them to be put to death. And ye shall
be hated of all men for my name's sake: but he that
endureth to the end shall be saved. But when they
persecute you in this city, flee ye into another: for verily I
say unto you, Ye shall not have gone over the cities of
Israel, till the Son of man be come. The disciple is not
above this master, nor the servant above his lord."
Matthew 10:16-24

We must "endure to till the end." Yah Jesus certainly doesn't promise us a "free ride" as so many people think. "For we wrestle not against flesh and blood, but against principalities, against powers, against the rulers of the darkness of this war, against spiritual *wickedness in high places." Ephesians 6:12o*

"Thou therefore endure hardness, as a good soldier of Jesus Christ. No man that

warmth entangled himself with the affairs of this life; that he may please him who

hath chosen him to be a soldier." II Timothy 2:3-4 "Beloved, when I gave all

diligence to write unto you of the common salvation, it was needful for me to

write unto you, and exhort you that ye should earnestly contend [to fight for] for

the faith which was once delivered unto the saints." Jude 3

Why should we as human's fight? The obvious answer is because God Yahweh wants us to. These and many other scriptures make God Yahweh will plain. But, many people ask, "Why would God the heavenly father want us to fight when he has already fought the battle for us.

But Christ as a son over his own house; whose house are

we, if we hold fast the confidence and the rejoicing of the

hope firm unto the end." Hebrews 3:6. "For we are made

partakers of Christ if we hold the beginning of us

confidence steadfast unto the end."

Hebrews 3:14

"If the world hate you, ye know that it hated me

before it hated you. If ye were of the world, the world

would love his own: but because ye are not of the
world, but I have chosen you out of the world, therefore
the world hateth you. Remember the word that I
said unto you, the servant is not greater than his lord.
If they have persecuted me, they will also persecute
you; if they have kept my saying, they will keep yours
also. But all these things will they do unto you for me
name's sake, because they know not him that sent me.
If I had not come and spoken unto them, they had not
had sin: but now they have no cloke for their sin."
John 15:18-22

Listen If the Leader in the Church Just stand up and tell it like it is.
Saints and non-Saints when be better prepare and equipped for
Spiritual Battel.

The gospel is not really being presented in full it is not 100 at all.
When have you ever heard any evangelist get up and say Listen
Saints and Non Saints can have salvation, but there is only one
condition, that you are totally committed, totally sold to Yahushua
Jesus Christ, you don't have any personal rights, you no longer
belong to yourself, you no longer have any right to anything at all.
You will become a servant. In essence you are signing your own
death warrant because Satan will hate you and try to kill you. You
ARE gaining eternal life and citizenship in heaven. You give up your
life here on earth to gain eternal life in heaven. With Yahweh
Yahushua and the Holy Spirit." How many preachers do you know

who present this? How many tracts in this world tell the simple truth? <u>NONE</u>! Why does Satan and the world hate Yah Jesus so much? Because once He came they "... now have no cloke meaning no covering for their sin's and sinful nature to hide it anymore it is out in the opening now for God and all to see once expose and God will expose you too." (vs. 23)

"[Jesus speaking] And this is the condemnation, that light

is come into the world, and men loved darkness rather

than light, because their deeds were evil."

John 3:19

"If any man come to me, and hate not his father, and mother, and wife, and

children, and brethren, and sisters, yea, and his own life also, he cannot be me

disciple. And whosoever doth not bear his cross, and come after me, cannot be

my disciple." Luke 14:26-27

"Then said Jesus unto his disciples, if any man will come after me, let him deny

himself, and take up his cross, and follow me. For whosoever will save his life

shall lose it: and whosoever will lose his life for my sake shall find it. For what is a man profited, if he shall gain the whole world, and lose his own soul? or what

shall a man give in exchange for his soul? For the Son of man shall come in the

glory of his Father with his angels; and then he shall reward every man according

to his works." Matthew 16:24-27

II Corinthians 6:9

People will say, "You're really coming across hard." God says in Isaiah:

"For my thoughts are not your thoughts, neither are your

ways my ways, saith the Lord. For as the heavens are

higher than the earth, so are my ways higher than your

ways, and my thoughts than your thoughts."

Isaiah 55:8-9

Many therefore of his disciples, when they had heard this said, this is a hard

saying; who can hear it? ... From that time many of his disciples went back, and

walked no more with him." John 6:60 & 66

"Blessed are they which are persecuted for righteousness'

sake: for theirs is the kingdom of heaven. Blessed are ye,

when men shall revile you, and persecute you, and shall say all manner of evil against you falsely, for my sake. Rejoice, and be exceeding glad: for great is your reward in heaven: for so persecuted they the prophets which were before you."
Matthew 5:10-12

"For I know this, that after my departing shall grievous wolves enter in among you, not sparing the flock. Also of your own selves shall men arise, speaking perverse things, to draw away disciples after them."
Acts 20:29-30

"For such are false apostles, deceitful workers, transforming themselves into the apostles of Christ. And no marvel; for Satan himself is transformed into an angel of light. Therefore, it is no great thing if his ministers also be transformed as the ministers of righteousness; whose end shall be according to their works."
II Corinthians 11:13-15

"Let the prophets speak two or three, and let the other judge." [Carefully weigh, evaluate, etc.]
I Corinthians 14:29

Be careful who you confide in, be wise, be alert to the Lord's guidance always. Our Lord

warned us: *"Lay hands suddenly on no man ..." I Timothy 5:22*

Wait to see the fruits of a person's life; wait until the Lord gives you a complete peace

with them.

"Beloved, believe not every spirit, but try the spirits whether they are of God:

because many false prophets are gone out into the world." I John 4:1

Remember, Satan and his demons will always try to deceive you. Especially in spiritual

Matters

He that loveth father or mother more than me is not

worthy of me: and he that loveth son or daughter more

than me is not worthy of me. And he that taketh not his

cross, and followeth after me, is not worthy of me."

Matthew 10:37-38 "... he that loseth his life for my sake

shall find it."

Matthew 10:39

I [Jesus] have yet many things to say unto you, but ye cannot bear them now.

How about it when he, the Spirit of truth, is come, he will guide you into all truth: for he shall not speak of himself; but whatsoever he shall hear, that shall he speak: and he will shew your things to come. He shall glorify me: for he shall receive of mine, and shall shew it unto you." John 16:12-14 "Whereof the Holy Spirit also is a witness to us: for after that he had said before, this is the covenant that I will make with them after those days, saith the Lord, I will put my laws into their hearts, and in their minds will I write them;" Hebrews 10:15-16.

The Holy Spirit will put thoughts into our minds, that is how He speaks to us and is witness to us. Satan can also flash thoughts into our minds, but remember, the Holy Spirit will confirm to your heart and spirit what is from Satan, and what is not. The Bible is our safeguard here. The Lord will never tell you anything that is not consistent with His word, the Bible. Also, if you are praying and talking with the Lord silently, Satan cannot read your mind and thus will not be able to put in thoughts that are in context with what is currently going on in your mind as you pray. This is another important reason why you must learn to control your mind so that it does not wander while you are in prayer and communion with the Lord Yah Jesus.

"I love them that love me; and those that seek me early shall find me." Proverbs

8:17

The literal translation of the Hebrew word for "early" means "diligently, with the implication of earnestness" according to Strong's Exhaustive Concordance of the Bible. You must seek such a relationship with the Lord diligently.

"The Spirit itself beareth witness with our spirit, that we are the children of God:"

Romans 8:16 "Wherefore as the Holy Ghost saith, today if ye will hear his voice,

Harden not your hearts, as in the provocation, in the day of temptation in the

wilderness:" Hebrews 3:8-9

"For though we walk in the flesh, we do not war after the flesh: (For the weapons of our warfare are not carnal, but mighty through God to the pulling down of strong holds;) Casting down imaginations, and every high thing that exalteth itself against the knowledge of God, and bringing into captivity every thought to the obedience of Christ." II Corinthians 10:5 "And be not conformed to this world: but be ye transformed by the renewing of your mind ..." Romans 12:2

Finally, brethren, whatsoever things are true, whatsoever things are honest, whatsoever things are just, whatsoever things are pure, whatsoever things are lovely, whatsoever things are of good report; if there be any virtue, and if there be any praise, think on these things." Philippians 4:8

This is another example of controlling our minds. We must literally re-train and renew

our minds as in Romans:

"And be not conformed to this world: but be ye transformed by the renewing of

your mind, that ye may prove what is that good, and acceptable, and perfect, will

of God." Romans 12:2

This takes time and persistence, and hard work!

"Put on therefore, as the elect of God, holy and beloved, bowels of mercies,

kindness, humbleness of mind, meekness, longsuffering;" Colossians 3:12

John 3:16 - For God so loved the world, that he gave his only begotten Son, that

whosoever believeth in him should not perish, but have everlasting life. — John

3:16

"God's children should not only learn to recognize authority; they should likewise be looking for those to whom they ought to be obedient. The centurion spoke to the Lord Jesus saying:

'I also am a man under authority, having under myself soldiers.' (Matt. 8:9)

He was truly a man who knew his and all authority. Today, even as Yahweh God upholds the whole universe with His authority, so He joins His children together through His authority. If any one of His children is independent and self-reliant, not subject to God's delegated authority, then that one can never accomplish the work of God on earth. Each and every child of God must look for some authority to obey so that he or she may be well coordinated with others. It is very sad to say, though, many have failed this point." Now when Daniel knew that the writing was signed, he went into his house; and his windows being open in his chamber toward Jerusalem, he kneeled upon his knees three times a day, and prayed, and gave thanks before his God, as he _did fore time."_ _Daniel 6:10_

_"_Likewise also these filthy dreamers defile the flesh, despise dominion, and speak evil of dignities. Yet Michael the archangel when contending with the devil he disputed about the body of Moses, durst not bring against him a railing accusation,

but said, 'The Lord rebuke thee.' But these speak evil of those things which they

know not ..." Jude verses 8-9

"Be sober, be vigilant; because your adversary the devil, as a roaring lion, walketh

about, seeking whom he may devour." II Peter 5:8

"Thou sealest up the sum, full of wisdom and perfect in beauty." _Ezekiel 28:12_

Wherewithal shall a young man cleanse his way? By taking heed thereto *according to thy word ... Thy word have I hid in mine heart, that I might not sin*

against thee." Psalm 119: 9 & 11

Vampires and werewolves have been legend for many years. Much has been written about them and many movies and stories have centered all around them. Unfortunately, most everyone believes they are simply "make-believe" fantasy creatures, and almost everything told about them is inaccurate. These creatures do exist. Let me define what I mean by war beasts and vampires, then lotus look at some interesting scriptural references.

"Behold, I was shapen in iniquity; and in sin did my mother conceive me." Psalm

51:5

Ever since the fall of Adam and Eve humans have been born sinful, and their physical bodies shaped in and peculiarly affected by iniquity. (Iniquity means wickedness.) Because of this the demons have great power over our physical bodies. People totally committed to Satan can and do ask certain demons to live in them that are capable of bringing about tremendous physical changes in their bodies. It is well known that demons can give humans unusual strength.

Remember the demoniac of Gadarah in Luke 8. Were beasts are produced by these demons. The demons bring about the physical changes in the person's body that change them into animal-like shapes and also gives them super-human strength and characteristics. There are some very interesting scriptures on this subject. Of course the term war animals or were beasts is not used as that is a fairly modern term. But let us look at the following:

"And I will give peace in the land ... and I will rid evil

beasts out of the land." Leviticus 26:6 "I will also send

wild beasts among you ..."

Leviticus 26:22

In these two references a clear distinction is made between evil beasts and wild beasts. God is here telling the Israelites that if they obey His commandments that He will rid the land of the Canaanites of evil beasts, but that if they do not keep His Commandments he will send in wild beasts to kill them. Earlier on when God gave Moses the law. He designated certain animals clean and unclean among both wild and domestic animals. So

evil beasts clearly mean something different from unclean beasts.

"[God speaking] the wild beasts of the field are mine ..." Psalm 50:11

There are many numerous references to wild beasts belonging to the Lord Yah Jesus, but never to evil beasts belonging to Him. Then we find a most interesting scripture in Ezekiel. Here, the Lord is instructing Ezekiel to go into the temple at Jerusalem to see the evil that was being practiced there. At this time the Israelites were practicing demon and Satan worship with all the perversions that accompany it.

"And he [God] said unto me, go in, and behold the

wicked abominations that they do here. So I went in and

saw; and behold every form of creeping things, and

abominable beasts, and all the idols of the house of Israel,

portrayed upon the wall round about."

Ezekiel 8:9-10

In a previously referenced scripture in I Corinthians 10:19-20, it is clearly stated that these

idols were images of the demons that were worshiped. I believe that the drawings which Ezekiel saw were not only of demons, but also of were beasts. Israel has been in Egypt forever 400 years prior to this time. The hieroglyphics found throughout Egypt contain drawings of creature's part human part beast, especially of human bodies with wolf heads. There are many references in scripture to show that the Israelites carried the Egyptian traditions and forms of worship with them.

References to evil beasts are also made in the New Testament. I believe the following scriptures are referring to what we call were beasts today. "One of themselves, even a prophet of their own, said, 'The Creations are always liars, evil beasts, slow bellies.' This witness is true

." Titus 1:12-13a

"Even as Sodom and Gomorrah, and the cities about

them in like manner, giving themselves over to

fornication, and going after strange flesh, are set forth

for an example, suffering the vengeance of eternal fire.

Likewise, also these filthy dreamers defile the flesh,

despise dominion, and speak evil of dignities

[demons]... But these speak evil of those things which

they know not: but what they know naturally, as brute

beasts, in those things they corrupt themselves. Woe

unto them! for they have gone in the way of Cain, and

ran greedily after the error of Balaam ... [The error of

Balaam was demon worship, specifically Baal.]"

Jude 7-11

There is an almost identical passage is found in II Peter 2:10-12. This passage shows how many men are corrupted and turned into beasts by lacking respect for and consorting with and worshiping demons. There is also clear reference to a special defiling of the flesh and a reference to "strange flesh. "Much is hidden in the scriptures and we must seek wisdom from the Lord to understand all this, but these scriptures make reference to the phenomenon of human beings literally turned into evil beasts with actual temporary physical changes brought about by demons.

Most people consider such things as werewolves, vampires and zombies pure fantasy. Christians need to understand that Satan and his servants are deadly serious about these creatures and that they do exist. The satanic activity in the Dark Ages was so intense because the light of the gospel of Yah Jesus was almost extinct. Witchcraft was rampant during that time until God brought the Reformation and the gospel was preached again.

The only accurate writings about the existence of were animals we have been able to find are translations of writings by a few German Christians during the start of the Reformation period. Sweet Yah Jesus told us that in the last days before His return that evil would increase tremendously, far more than that of the Dark Ages. Satan is on the move and we are going to see more and more manifestations of his power. The explosion of occult movies, satanic rock music, satanic role playing fantasy games, occult literature, Eastern religions and lukewarm uncommitted Christians should give us a good indication of the times we are in.

"[Jesus speaking about the last days before His return.]

For then shall be great tribulation, such as was not since

the beginning of the world to this time, no nor ever shall

be. And except those days should be shortened, there

should no flesh be saved: but for the elect's sake those?

days shall be shortened ... For there shall arise false

Christs, and false prophets, and shall shew great signs and

wonders; insomuch that, if it were possible, they shall

deceive the very elect."

Matthew 24:21-24

"My soul is among lions: and I lie even among them that are set on fire, even the

sons of men whose teeth are spears and arrows ..." Psalm 57:4
Now Demons can and do manifest in a physical form. The forms they chose to take can range from exquisite beauty to horrifying ugliness. Demons can also manifest in a physical appearance identical to an existing human being. These demons are frequently referred to by Satanists as changelings, incubi, or Doppler-gangers. Gang bagger evil twins; spiritual clone's We must also stand against these the same as any demon, in the name of Jesus "For such are false apostles, deceitful workers, transforming

themselves into the apostles of Christ. And no marvel; for Satan himself is transformed into an angel of light. Therefore, it is no great thing if his ministers also be transformed as the ministers of righteousness; whose end shall be according to their works."

II Corinthians 11:13-15

"For there are certain men crept in unawares, who were before of old ordained to

this condemnation, ungodly men, turning the grace of our God into

lasciviousness, and denying the only Lord God, and our Lord Jesus Christ."

"Rebuke not an elder, but entreat him as a father; and the

younger men as brethren; the elder women as mothers; the

younger as sisters, with all purity."

I Timothy 5:1

The word entreat means to ask earnestly, beseech; implore, with respect. Never forget that Yah Jesus loves these people and died for them just the same as He did for you and me. Your purpose is not to expose them, but to control them and get them saved.

"When ye come together ... If any man speaks in an

unknown tongue, let it be by two or at the most by three,

and that by course; and let one interpret. But if there be no

interpreter, let him keep silence in the church; and let him

speak to himself, and to God."

I Corinthians 14:26-28

Three other scriptures most churches overlook are: "Beloved, believe not every spirit, but try the spirits whether they are of God: because many false prophets are gone out into the world. Hereby know ye the Spirit of God: Every spirit that confessed that Jesus Christ is come in the flesh is of God: And every spirit that confessed not that Jesus Christ is come in the fleshes not of God: and this is that spirit of antichrist, whereof ye have heard that it should come; and even now already is it in the world.

" I John 4:1-3"And he said, take heed that ye be not deceived: for many shall come in my name..." Luke 21:8"Not every one that saith unto me, Lord, Lord, shall enter into the kingdom of heaven; but he that doeth the will of my Father which is in heaven. Many will say to me in that day, Lord, Lord, have we not prophesied in thy name? and in thane have cast out devils? and in thy name done many wonderful works? And then will I profess unto them, I never knew you: depart from me, ye that work of iniquity." Matthew 7:21-23

This seems to be one of the areas of greatest confusion amongst Christians. Satanists can and do use the name of Yah Jesus. They can teach and preach about Yah Jesus, they can use the name of Yahushua Jesus in prayer, etc. The scriptures just quoted in Luke and Matthew clearly show this. The one thing they can't do is pass the test given in I John 4. They cannot look you square in the eye and say, "Yah Jesus Christ who is God, who came in the flesh, died on the Calvary and shed his blood for his righteous chosen one of God and three days later arose from the grave and now sits at the right-hand of God the Father, and he Yahushua is God as well and always has been before the beginning of time. This is the only way man could be saved if God himself came down and did no mere mortal man could do, the flesh was corrupted. This Yah Jesus is my Lord and Savior and Master."

Oh, they can say "Yah Jesus saved me." But which Jesus are they talking about? Yah Jesus Himself said that many would come claiming to be Him. Many false ones even Satan has one the Antichrist the son of perdition will soon be on the earthly seen as well. We are almost there according to revelations and Daniels in the bible. They the demons and witches and occult elect of Satan can also read or repeat a confession or profession of faith in Yah Jesus Christ. They can and do read the scriptures.

If you ask them if Jesus Christ who came in the flesh is their Savior, they can lie and say "Yes." But they cannot, with their own mouth, make the declaration as given above. God gave us a test to use, dear brothers and sisters in Christ. Let us use God's word. Satanists build credibility within the Christian churches in many ways, depending upon the particular church. They are regular attenders. They can be counted upon to always be ready and willing to help in any project. Not only do they build credibility in this way and honor status, but they also get to know the church and its members all about them witch us deadly for them if they carnal mined in the Lord. It doesn't take long for them to find out who is truly committed to Christ and who is not.

Money is another big tool they use. If the church is a large and wealthy one they give regularly, gradually increasing the amounts they give until they are one of the main supporter of the church financially. In small churches where the members are mostly poor, they do not flash around a lot of money, but gradually and carefully increase their giving until many of the programs within the church become dependent upon their financial support. That way they can control and rule over the church either to turn it into a Satanic church or destroy it by codependency on them the witchcraft folks etc. and Satan. Of course The Brotherhood who is the biggest witchcraft sect out there provides the money they give, and money talks!!! Unfortunately, this is true even in our Christian churches. Rarely will you find poor people on the board of directors of any church.

"Praying always with all prayer and supplication in the Spirit, and watching

thereunto with all perseverance and supplication for all saints;"
Ephesians 6:18

Also once the prayer base of the church has been destroyed, the Satanists are free to do about anything they want. This is also how they destroy an inadvisable person they befriend you support you give you gifts witches do this a lot and give you food. They must stand there and witness you eat or drank some of the food before they go. So take heed to that. Also one of the easiest things to use is rumors. Gossip is Satan's prime tool

. Very few people are strong enough not to pass along a rumor they have heard. Satanists can easily destroy the credibility of the pastor and the true Christians within church by starting rumors. All church leaders are urge to be very careful. Never go alone to the home of a member of the church of the opposite sex to help or counsel them. You can be framed so easily. Even if you did nothing unseemly or wrong, who can prove it? Many a pastor's career have been destroyed by just such set-ups. I Thessalonians 5:22 says, "Abstain from all appearance of evil." Every Christian would do well to carefully follow that scripture.

Stop All Accurate Teaching About Satan

"Lest Satan should get an advantage of us: for we are not ignorant of his devices."

II Corinthians 2:11

"My people are destroyed for lack of knowledge: because thou hast rejected knowledge, I will also reject thee, that thou shalt be no priest to me: seeing thou hast forgotten the law of thy God, I will also forget thy children." Hosea 4:6"Be sober, be vigilant; because your adversary the devil, as a roaring lion, walketh about, seeking whom he may devour." I Peter 5:8"And this is the condemnation, that light is come into the world, and men loved darkness rather than light, because their deeds were evil." John 3:19One of the major goals of Satan and his servants is to prevent any teaching about him or his activities. As long as people remain ignorant about Satan he is relatively unhindered in anything he chooses to do. Satanists are always commanded to prevent any teaching about Satan within the churches they attend.

The excuses are many. They say that any teaching about Satan gives glory to him, this is a good been used a lot through the years, this takes people's minds off of the God, tempts people to turn to Satan, etc., etc., ad infinitum. God's word clearly says and teaches much about Satan, and warns us that if we are ignorant about our enemy he will surely gain an advantage over us. One simple incantation by a high Satanist will assign a demon to every person attending the church in which he is involved. The purpose of the demon is to stand guard and then stand anyone says anything about Satan, to beam thoughts into the person's mind that he or she should not be listening to anything about Satan. Beware, the very church members who complain the loudest about any teaching about

Satan and his tactics, will probably turn out to be Satanists themselves

Direct Attacks by Witchcraft Against Key Members of the Church

This is another reason why prayer is so important. Any pastor and church leaders and or church members who are really taking a stand for the Lord and against Satan will come under tremendous attack by witchcraft. They will be afflicted with all sorts of physical illness, difficulties in concentrating, confusion, fatigue, difficulties in praying, etc. The leaders of any church must be continuously upheld in prayer and interceded for by the members of the congregation. Once such a prayer base is lost, the pastor and leaders face these attacks alone. Often they are overcome.

That is why Paul asked his fellow Christians to pray for him at the end of almost every letter he wrote. The incredible number of powerless, dead Christian churches in our land today is a testimony to the success of Satan's carefully planned tactics. Our prayer is that every Christian reading these words will go to the Yah Lord in prayer and seek guidance as to how to fight such attacks within his or her own church

Proof Satan and his Demons and Occult Elect of Satan Make Man Sick and Good heals.

And he Yah Jesus] came down with them, and stood in the plain, and the company of his disciples, and a great multitude of people out of all Judaea and Jerusalem, and from the sea coast of Tyre and Sidon, which came to hear him, and to be healed of their diseases; and they that were vexed with unclean spirits: and they were healed." Luke 6:17-18 Note the clear distinction made here that some of the illnesses were healed, and some were healed as a result of the unclean spirits being cast out. "And in that same hour he [Yah Jesus] cured many of their infirmities and plagues, and of evil spirits; and unto many that were blind he gave sight." Luke 7:21Again, the same distinction is made. There are two clear cases also given in Luke which demonstrate the same point — that is, some diseases are purely physical, and some are caused by demons.

"And as he [Jesus] was yet a coming, the devil threw him down, and tare him.

And Jesus rebuked the unclean spirit, and healed the child, and delivered him

again to his father." Luke 9:42 "And he [Jesus] arose out of the synagogue, and

entered into Simon's house. And Simon's wife's mother was taken with a great

fever; and they besought him for her. And he stood over her, and rebuked the

fever; and it left her: and immediately she arose and ministered unto them." Luke

4:38-39

The emphasized portions show the clear difference. In the first case Jesus healed by

rebuking the unclean spirit, in the second He headed by rebuking the physical fever.

Demons can, and do, cause illness. Not all illness is demonic, but a significant amount is. We must remember that physical as well as spiritual death was the result of ADAM AND EVE fall. The alteration in our physical bodies caused by sin makes us vulnerable to an array of physical illnesses. The Yahushua has taught me much in this area. Demons are expert in handling bacteria and viruses and do cause much illness by placing these into human bodies, but they can also do damage directly Demons tear apart a physical body on the molecular level. They do this in such a way that devastating damage can be done to the various organs without altering the appearance of the cellular structures under our microscopes.

 The damage they do usually requires treatment with physical medicines, nutrition, etc., but the physician can know only by direct revelation from the Yah Jesus, what is really wrong with such a patient and what treatment to use. Few Christian physicians are willing to take the risk of depending on the

Yahweh so completely. I am not advocating treating a patient without all the appropriate diagnostic tests, but every physician, whether he will admit it or not, sees an uncomfortable number of cases in which all the diagnostics do not give the answer as to what is wrong with the patient. In these cases, it is the responsibility of the physician to specially seek the Lord's guidance with fasting and prayer.

I think we should discuss here one of the most common problems afflicting the human

race — DEPRESSION. Much is written about depression in the Bible.

"Why art thou cast down, O my soul? and why art thou disquieted in me? Hope thou in God: for I shall yet praise him for the help of his countenance. O my God, my soul is cast down within me: therefore, will I remember thee from the land of

ROSALIND SOLOMON

Jordan, and of the Hermonites, from the hill Mizar." Psalm 42:5-6

There are a multitude of references in the Psalms and other places to <u>depression.</u> This battle is real, and we are very human! I am so thankful that the <u>Yahushua included such scriptures in the Bible.</u> Look at the following verses: "<u>Awake, why sleepest thou, O Lord?</u> <u>arise, cast us not off forever. Where fore hidest thou thy face, and</u> <u>forgettest our affliction and our oppression? For our souls bowed</u> <u>down to the dust: our belly cleaveth unto the earth." Psalm 44:23-</u> <u>25</u>If any true born-again believer tries to tell me that he has never felt the emotions expressed in the above two sections quoted, I would have to say that either he has never taken a stand for God and thus become involved in spiritual warfare, or he is lying!

Look at the great honesty with which Paul the apostle wrote:

"For we would not, brethren, have you ignorant of us

trouble which came to us in Asia, that we were pressed

out of measure, above strength, insomuch that we

despaired even of life: But we had the sentence of death

in ourselves, that we should not trust in ourselves, but in

God which raised the dead."

II Corinthians 1:8-9

<u>There are many causes of depression. Unfortunately,</u> too many people involved in deliverance ministries say that all depression is demonic. I think this is because we humans always are looking for the easy way out of any situation. If all depression is demonic in origin the solution is simple, cast out the demon and presto, the depression is gone! It has been my experience that the majority of cases of serious depression that I have seen have not been the

result of a demon of depression indwelling in the person. The most frequent cause of serious depression that I have seen is a direct result of an almost complete lack of mind control. God's word clearly tells us that we are to take captive every thought to make it obedient to Yah Jesus Christ. (II Cor. 3:5.) Seriously depressed people (including Christians) almost never obey this direct command from the God.

They allow any thought to stay in their mind which Satan and or his demons chose to put there. They never stop to evaluate how accurate their thoughts are with the reality of their situation, or with the situation in the light of God's word. They accept all thoughts as being from themselves, in short, they are lazy! They have allowed their minds to slip into lazy passivity and in such a state they come under tremendous emotional torment by demonic forces. The fight to regain control of your mind is one of the most difficult battles you will ever engage in, but it will be well worth the effort. I

Note how David was doing this in Psalm 42 where he says "...I will yet praise the Lord ..." He was using his will to overcome the depressive thoughts in his soul (mind) and declaring that he would praise the Lord. Praise plays a very important part in overcoming depression. Please note my own experience feeling oppress and depress by the enemy. I would sing to God and it help me and eventually deliver me from it. Other common sources of depression are a major loss, such as of a loved one, physical illness and weakness, big adverse changes in life circumstances and, of course, from pure exhaustion — especially in people involved in spiritual warfare.

Those of us involved in spiritual warfare need to be continually sensitive and obedient to the Yah Jesus Lord's leading in this area. When the Yah Jesus commands you to stop and rest you had better obey no matter how unnecessary you may think the request at the moment, or you will no doubt get shutdown quickly. By this I mean, you will suffer either serious physical or emotion difficulties, (especially in the area of relationships with other people) or you may fall into error and be deceived because you can no longer be as alert as you need to be.

Too many people forget that they are still human with human weaknesses and limitations. If we let the Lord guide us in these areas, we will avoid much difficulty. Some of the most powerful demons I have ever encountered have come into a person as a result of incest within a family and the various sexual perversions Marine Kingdom Demons Incubus and succubus and a Whole Host of demons. — especially <u>sadomasochism</u> which has become so popular today through heavy metal Rock music and R and B Music and Country music as well.

<u>These powerful demons often are of a class of demons that are able to inhabit all three</u>

Areas of the human at once — body and soul and spirit <u>*"Behold my servant, whom I uphold; mine elect, in whom*</u>

<u>*my soul delighteth; I have put my spirit upon him: he*</u>

<u>*shall bring forth judgment to the Gentiles. He shall not*</u>

<u>*cry, nor lift up, nor cause his voice to be heard in the*</u>

<u>*street. A bruised reed shall he not break, and the smoking*</u>

<u>*flax shall he not quench: he shall bring forth judgment*</u>

<u>*unto truth. He shall not fail nor be discouraged, till he*</u>

have set judgment in the earth: and the isles shall wait for

his law." Isaiah 42:1-4 "My little children, let us not love

in word, neither in tongue; but indeed and in truth." I

John 3:18

And these signs shall follow them that believe ... they shall lay
hands on the sick,

and they shall recover." Mark 16:17-18

"Is any sick among you? Let him call for the elders of the church;
and let them

pray over him, anointing him with oil in the name of the Lord: And
the prayer of

faith shall save the sick, and the Lord shall raise him up..." James
5:14-15

he people; (and they were all with one accord in

Solomon's porch). And of the rest durst no man join

himself to them: but the people magnified them."

Acts 5:11-13"And Jesus rebuked the devil; and he departed out of
him:

and the child was cured from that very hour. Then came

the disciples to Jesus apart, and said, Why could not we

cast him out? Jesus said unto them ... this kind goeth not

out but by prayer and fasting."

Matthew 17:18-19 & 21

SPELLS, INCANTATIONS, HEXES & CURSES

All of these accomplish the same purpose — that is, to summon a demon or demons to perform a given action. Frequently incantations are in poetic form, they are multitudinous and have been passed down from generation to generation. They are usually spoken aloud (remember, demons cannot read the human mind), but often are spoken by the witch's spirit into the spirit world which is not audible to the physical ear. The term "Placing a spell, hex, or curse on someone," refers to the act of calling up a demon and then sending it to the person to perform certain influences or damage.

 ALL spells, etc., are accomplished by demons, even the so-called "good" ones such as those stimulating love in a person, etc. Another term used especially in some other countries is "bewitched," that is, someone who is under the influence or control of demons sent by a witch. The more powerful witches do not have to use long and complex incantations. They simply communicate with the demons directly in the spirit world, or through their "guiding spirit.

PEOPLE WHO SMOKE AND CANNOT AND CANNOT HER THE GOSPEL AND ON DRUGS OR DEANK A LOT A DURKER. THYE HAVE THE WITTCHES LENT OR COTTON MIX WITH PLAM OIL GOGGING THEIR EAR; S SO THEY CANNOT HERA YOU WHEN YOU SAY THEY COULD DIE FROM THESES THINGS OR WHEN YOU TRYING TO GET THEM TO ACCECT Yah Jesus to receive salvation

SO PRAY THIS BEFORE YOU GO OUT TO EVANGELIZE OR BEFORE YOU TALK TO A FAMILY MEMBER

Remove the Witches Lent and Cotton in Lam oil out Prayer

Father Yahweh I ask you to burn the witches lent and or cotton with the palm oil or whatever they using to glug this person _____ Ear's up from hearing me or anyone else about their sin or the gospel or salvation. In Yah Jesus name I also ask You Father Yahweh God to allow the Blood of Yahushua Jesus flow through their ears and whole being and clean out the dross and poison left over. So the demons and the witches won't have a root to come back in them and harm them. So they can continue to hear the Gospel and function in you and do your Kingdom work and their also their destiny and so they can be equipping to stand against Satan and his kingdom with your Power Father Yahweh and Yah Jesus and the Holy Spirit power in Yah Jesus name. Allow the Holy spirit to come down and take over them now and forever more in Yah Jesus name

Where do evil thoughts come from?

Ask yourself this Does Satan really put them there? I think he does, because they just seem to come out of the blue into my head without any effortlessness on my part. In many cases, how are we going to deal with this?

A lot of times, the Satan truly often do place and drop and put evil thoughts in our head. Satan even will incite us to do evil thing's called sin. Think of Judas, the one who portrayed Yah Jesus for example, Judas had made a secret arrangement and agreement just to betray Yah Jesus to His enemies. When Judas went to go tell them where they could find Yah Jesus, the Bible says that "Satan entered into him" (John 13-27). But the ground was already prepared for Satan to work in Judas' heart and mind. Even though he was part of Yahushua Jesus' _twelve disciples, Judas_ did not at all believe that Yah Jesus was the Savior sent from God Yahweh nor that he was God in the Flesh to save us from our sins. This is a true fact, the Bible says that Judas "was a thief; as keeper of the money bag (_for the disciples),_ he used to help himself to what was put into it_" (John 12:6)._ And Yah Jesus knew it and let him do it because Yah knew Judas purpose was to betray him. The lesson is here being very clear The farther we get and are from God, the more vulnerable we will be to Satan's attacks.

Let's not be like Judas, but make certain of your commitment to Yah Jesus Christ. If you've never done so, turn to Him Yah and by faith ask Him to come into your heart and life. Then ask Him Yah to fill your mind with His truth and His Spirit every day. The Bible says, "Submit yourselves, then, to God Yahweh. Resist the devil, and he will flee from you" (_James 4:7)._ Not all evil thoughts come directly from Satan, however. Often they come from within – from our own sinful hearts. Just remember this as well.

Cancel evil thoughts from Satan and his demon's prayer

Father in the name of Yah Jesus I cancel any and all thoughts coming in my commutation channel from   Satan and his cohorts and _Demons Who Are Interfering in my mind_ with the Blood of the Lamb Yah Jesus and the affect and manifestation of these thoughts in Yah Jesus name. That will try and cause me to do evil and think evil in Yah Jesus name and to stop them and Satan from bringing division in my mind and division between you and me God. In Yah Jesus name. I refuse to allow such thoughts to compromise me with you Father and the Holy Spirit and Yahushua in Yah Jesus name. Father Yahweh of Heaven and Earth please wash my mind in The blood of Yah Jesus this day and every day in Yah Jesu name.

I Thank Yahweh God and the Holy Spirit and Yah Jesus to be able to place this book together. I also thank Apostle Grace Anderson for Allowing me to use some of her prayer's for this 3rd prayer book I have done. All of the Scripture are from King James Bible. God bless you.

Made in the USA
Middletown, DE
17 May 2025